POEMS *from the* HEART *for* HOPE *and* HEALING

For Those Who Have Experienced Estrangement from a Loved One

CLAIRE L. CUNNING

ARCHWAY
PUBLISHING

Archway Publishing books may be ordered through booksellers or by contacting:

Archway Publishing
1663 Liberty Drive
Bloomington, IN 47403
www.archwaypublishing.com
844-669-3957

ISBN: 978-1-6657-0061-0 (sc)
ISBN: 978-1-6657-0062-7 (e)

Library of Congress Control Number: 2020925138

Print information available on the last page.

Archway Publishing rev. date: 1/7/2021

A NOTE FROM THE AUTHOR

In my quest to find relief from the pain that comes from the struggles of estrangement, I wrote this heartfelt collection of poems. I have found in my experience over the last 10 years, there is no rational logic for the rise and fall of my grief. I may be at peace one day, and angry and confused the next day. I have divided my poems into sections so that the reader may "pop" in and out of a section as needed, for grief certainly does not show its cutting edges in any particular order. I do not, in any way, consider myself to be an expert on this complex subject of estrangement. Nor am I able to counsel or advise anyone professionally. What I mostly want to convey is that these poems were written from my heart to give the reader some comfort in knowing that they are not alone in their own quest for hope and healing.

HURT *and* GRIEF

GRIEF

Grief sneaks up on you
In such a creepy way.
It screams from your insides,
"Won't you come out and play?"
I hear myself crying out,
"Please don't stay!"

But
It taunts me and says,
"Is that all you've got?
No more tears for the one
You have lost?

"You have much more sadness
You're holding inside.
Don't you need just
Another good cry?"

Oh, wretched grief,
Don't haunt me like this!
It's taken me years of suffering
To crawl out of the abyss.
I feel you creeping back in
The way you like to smother.
Crawl back where you came from
Before you destroy another.

NOT SORRY

I'm sorry I wasn't the mother you needed me to be;
I'm sorry for what I did or didn't do.
I'm sorry if I did something wrong;
It wasn't done intentionally.

I'm sorry you think you can't include me
In this life you so carefully enjoy.
I'm sorry for missing that little man
Who once gave me so much joy.

I'm sorry the years are drifting by
And I just can't make you see
The mother you have is still right here,
Crouched on bended knee.

She's crying, "I'm not sorry for having a son;
I've always been proud of him."
She's praying someday he'll open his arms
And let her come back in.

For no one knows your cries like she does,
And no one knows your heart.
So I'm sorry if I'm not giving up on you;
I just want a brand-new start.

PONDERINGS

Why have you become so cold?
The days go by without a word, a thought, a text.
I'm nervous to think
What will be next.
What has happened to your soul?
That has allowed you
To become so cold.

I see you as you were
On days gone by.
Where is my little guy?
I wouldn't ask if it weren't true.
I don't know how to reach out to you!

The days, the months, the years go past;
Yet I'm not permitted to ask.
What has become of my loving child
Who brought me flowers growing wild?

Where is the one
Who brought me breakfast in bed
On Mother's Day?
The one who begged me to play
Just one more game?

I can't imagine where
That child has gone.
And I can't imagine
Where I went wrong.

There are some who think
I should just let you go.
But as your mother, I cannot do that,
As you should know.

So for now, I will just wait
And hope and pray
That your eyes will be opened
On some blessed day.

PARALYZED

You've left me paralyzed.
When I see you,
I just freeze.
It's so numbing,
I fall to my knees.

Numb from the loss of you.
Numb from the pain.
Numb from the idea of never seeing you again.
Numb from trying and getting nowhere.
Numb from knowing you just don't care.

It's a paralyzing feeling
When in limbo—
Not knowing which way to move
Or what feelings to show.

It's paralyzing when you live
With your heart on your sleeve
And others have no idea
Of your heart's raging siege.

And some days, it's an effort
To just maneuver through
Another day
Of not seeing you.

If you only knew how
This numbness takes its toll.
It is paralyzing!
It's so cold.

GUILTY

I'm guilty of letting you go,
Even though it's a place
I haven't wanted to go.
I'm guilty of shutting you out.
This is the way you must want it;
I have no doubt.

I'm guilty of tucking you away
In the deepest crevices
Of my heart.
It's the safest place to be
When it's so torn apart.

I'm guilty of feeling guilt
Because I have finally quit trying.
I tried my best,
But your love you keep denying.

I'm guilty of loving you unconditionally,
When you don't love me without conditions.
I'm guilty of blocking you out of my mind
When your name somebody mentions.

How dare you make me feel guilty
For yearning for what others have with
Their loved ones.
You are the one who should feel guilty
For getting rid of your mom.

IN MY MIND

In my mind,
I'm just like any other mother.
My son and I really love each other.

In my mind,
We hug when we greet.
He's the same boy I raised,
Who was so sweet.

In my mind,
I still find comfort in his smile.
I can still stop by
And talk for a while.

In my mind,
He's that boy I've always known,
And I still tease him
About how much he's grown.

In my mind,
We laugh at our own jokes
And talk of days past.
We attend picnics and parties,
But those days don't last.

In my mind,
I know you are still there
Somewhere.
In my mind,
I just want you to care!

In my mind, I think,
How do you dare
Turn your back on the one
Who's always been there?

But my mind plays tricks on me;
You are not here.
These are just memories
I hold dear.

In my mind,
You too hope for the reunion
That I am craving.
In my mind,
I hope that these thoughts
Are worth saving.

MEMORIES

I have scars on my heart
Where once there was joy—
Memories of my once
Happy little boy.
Memories seep out
And slip down my cheeks,
Leaving scars on my heart
That make me feel weak.

Memories seem to have a life
Of their own.
I wish sometimes,
They'd just let me alone.
Memories appear when you
Least expect them,
Destroying a perfectly good day
If you let them.

Memories pull you away
From what is real,
And all your dreams
They try to steal.
Memories can bring us hope
From days we used to know.
But for me, they leave scars
Of a life not long ago.

WAVES OF EMOTIONS

My grief comes in waves
As they roll to the shore.
They peak and crash and die
With the ocean's roar.

Some days are quiet
As my mind reflects.
Others are long and anxious,
For I just can't forget.

For my memories still flow
With the ebb and tide,
And my sadness still lingers
As far as the ocean is wide.

But I also feel some warmth
As the sun sparkles through the sand,
For I sometimes see glimmers of my son,
Who is now a grown man.

Why has he chosen a path without his mother,
The one who loves him quite like no other?
Only he can answer a question like this.
So for now, I just hang on
To the side of the abyss.

ESTRANGEMENT

Why don't I matter to you?
It's so insane!
I'm your mother, for heaven's sake,
And I'm not going to take the blame
For this separation
That has a name.

Estrangement is a terrible hurt.
I can't think of anything worse.
You are absent, but you are really here.
With each day of loss,
Your face seems to disappear.

At one time in your life,
I was *all* that mattered.
But at this date in time,
It seems all that has been shattered.

Does it matter to you at all
That I was at your beck and call?
I would have done anything for you,
But we have hit a brick wall.
Does it not matter to you
That I long for your attention?
That I cry for you in the night,
And do I dare to mention?

The memories of you just won't
Go away.
You're my son,
And I need them to stay.

How can your parents not matter to you?
Do you have an idea
Of what you have put us through?

Every car that goes by,
I swear it is you.
Every creak of the door
Might be you coming through.

Every time the phone rings,
My heart starts to sing.
Is it you, my son?
What hope you could bring!

ANGER and DENIAL

RIGHTS

What gives you the right
To throw us out like an old shoe,
To ignore our pleas, our texts, our love?
What the hell is wrong with you?

What right do you have to accept gifts
With no thought of a reply?
Maybe I should start repaying you
An eye for an eye.

What right do you have to keep our grandchildren
Neatly tucked away
As if they are fragile dolls
Without an opinion,
Without a say?

We are missing them
As they grow and learn and change.
Do you think this is your right?
Is this some sort of wicked game?

And what of the children's rights—
Don't they have a say?
How petty to use them as pawns
In this nasty game you play!

No one should have the right to deny us
Of time spent with those we love.
The only One who can do that
Is watching from high above.

And He must be shaking His head right now
And asking in vain,
"Why can't you just all get along?"
There's way too much pain!

So the next time you say,
"We are just too busy"
Or "We don't have the time,"
Tell it to the Lord above,
For your parents may
Soon be out of time.

THE FIXER

I am a *Fixer* but I can't fix this.
I cannot fix your attitude.
I cannot fix your
Indifference.

I cannot fix the pain you inflict on me.
I cannot fix the loss of a family I never see.
I can't fix all the days that have been lost.
I can't fix the heartbreak that you have cost.

I can't bring back the holidays where you weren't present.
I can't relive birthdays where you were absent.
I can't miss you or my grandchildren any more than I do.
And I can't fix the fact that I still love you.

But I can fix myself
and the thoughts that I'm feeling.
I can fix those anxious emotions
when my head starts reeling.

I'm going to fix my mind
On the road ahead.
Of new places to see
And new paths to tread.

I'm going to think of the friends
That I have made.
And of the family
That has stayed and prayed...
With me.

The saddest part in all of this,
Is that a broken heart
Is the hardest to fix.

TRIGGERS

I saw your best friend today.
He hugged me and said,
"It's been years!"
"How's my best friend?" he asked.
I replied, "It's been years."
And then came the tears.

A neighbor boy ran by our house today
And stopped to say hello.
He's become a young man now,
Someone I used to know.

He asked, "How's my old neighbor guy?"
"I don't know," I said,
Turning my head in reply.
I could hardly say the words aloud:
"He hasn't been home in a while."
And that's when I started to cry.

I saw a high school friend last night,
Coming out of a store.
I turned my head so she wouldn't see me
For I knew what was in store.

"How's your son?" she will ask.
And I was not quite sure
I was ready to tackle this question.
So I headed for the door.

I shuffled to my car
With my head held down.
I had a desperate feeling
To just get out of town.

I can't handle another trigger!
Not today!
Sometimes it's much easier
To just run away.

TUG OF WAR

There's a tug of war going on
Inside my head,
And sometimes these thoughts of mine
Just cause me to dread
Another day without a reply,
Another day to wonder why.

Should I call you on the phone,
Or shall I continue to let you alone?
Should I send you a text
Or just give it a rest?

Should I send you a birthday card?
Can I stop by your workplace?
These questions are not hard
Nor are they out of place!

So the tug of war goes on:
Should I drive by your home
In hopes the grandkids are out?
Should I knock on the door
And get kicked out?
But when you are estranged,
These questions make us weary
Because the answer we get
Can be seen quite clearly.

I'm not going to get an answer,
So I'm not going to sit by the phone.
And I'm not going to waste another moment
Sitting here all alone.

The thing is,
This tug of war is not normal
For a parent to endure.
So I'm going to end this struggle.
I can't do it anymore!

I'M DIVORCING
MY SON

I'm divorcing my son.
Okay, you have won!
I'll take the good memories.
You can have what's left.
I'll take a few photos;
You can have the rest.

I give up on visitation.
You've made it way too unacceptable.
It's hard to see someone who isn't accessible.
I can't see your children without an appointment.
You have taken away all the enjoyment.

So for what it's worth,
I'm divorcing you!

I hope you are happy,
Just you and your little fam ...
Think about what you are doing.
Stand up, and be a man.

You know I'll always love you,
But I'm divorcing your disrespect.
I'm divorcing your indifference.
I'm divorcing your neglect.

I'm divorcing your life
And its constant coldness.
I hope you don't catch a chill
While living among this.

I am *not* divorcing your children!
They have done nothing wrong
Except to follow your lead,
Which is all so wrong!

I hope you realize
I've always been there.
All you've had to do
Is just give a care.

FAMILY IS NOT EVERYTHING

Family may be everything to some,
But not for me.

We are a family that is broken.
It needs lots of repair.
This merry-go-round of emotions
Isn't getting us anywhere.

Family is not everything
When some don't know how to play.
The rules that they make
Keep us all at bay.

I just want to see my grandkids—
Such a simple request.
But the hands that deal the cards
Won't give it a rest.

"You can't see them—
Not today.
We are way too busy;
Maybe another day."
But that day never comes,
And so it replays.

Meanwhile, our grandkids are growing
By leaps and bounds
While you haven't had the decency
To bring them around.

It's heartbreaking to visualize;
They've grown up before our eyes.
Soon, someday, you'll realize
You weren't very wise.

So appreciate your family
If they are your everything.
Not all of us have the luxury
Of the joy that it can bring.

No, family is not everything
When you are not included.
I would give anything
Not to be excluded.

WHAT ABOUT THE CHILDREN?

What about the children?
What about us?
Is this the way God wants it to be—
You against us?

"Why can't I see my nana or my pappy?
Did I do something to make them unhappy?
I don't understand why I don't see them as much.
I surely miss my grandma's soft touch."

"I miss my pappy's strong hands
Helping me to throw and catch,
Teaching me how to play checkers.
I wonder what will be next?"

"I bet they both miss me.
I bet they miss my kisses.
I bet Nana wants me to taste her cookies.
I know these are their wishes."

"I miss the stories I heard from Nana's lap.
I miss the rides on Pappy's back.
I miss playing baseball in his big backyard.
No one can throw a baseball like he can.
He thinks I'm a star!"

"I believe that Pappy misses me too.
I helped him wash his truck, Old Red.
And even though he might not show it,
He liked it when
I tucked us both in bed."

"I'm just a kid, but
I know when something's not right.
I know when something's out of place.
It seems that the ones I look up to
Are doing this out of spite!"

"I wish I were old enough
To make up my own mind
Because the way you adults treat each other
Is far too unkind!"

STANDOFF

So I guess we are in a standoff—
Or is it a standstill?
Take your pick
If you will.

No one is talking
Or making a move.
It's like a game of chess,
And no one wants to lose.

But we've already both lost:
You a mother, me a son.
And this is for what?
Because you can't decide to forgive or forget—
Which one?

And I don't know what to apologize for.
So we remain in this place
I've come to abhor.

Another hour, another day, another week
The same as before.
We seem to be in a dead heat,
And I don't even know what for?

In this game of life we play,
There are winners and losers.
But neither of us have won.
You lost a mother
And me a son.

I think it's time to call a truce
And admit defeat,
Even though a victory
Would be so sweet
(For both of us).

I don't profess to know what's ahead ...
I just know it seems this standoff
Will never end.

DISAPPEARING ACT

I hope you're happy in this new life that
You've found
Despite the fact you've left us
With questions all around.

You've left all of us
With no thought or regard—
Not just your mom and dad,
But the rest of your family too.
They've been hit hard.

Everyone is wondering,
What shall we do?
I do not know what to tell them;
Do you?

Is it so hard
To answer a text or send a card,
To answer the phone
Or show some concern?

What has caused this absence in our lives?
It's hard for me to believe
You can just ignore all our cries
With no replies!

Where have you been?
We all want to know.
You've missed picnics and parties and reunions.
You're a no-show.

Are we to pretend you just don't exist?
It sure has become easy for you to do this!

People who know both you and me
Can't believe you can disappear so easily.
It's hard for me to answer them
About your existing welfare

Except to say, "You're lucky!
Your kids actually care!"

HOPE *and* HEALING

HOPE

I hope you're happy;
I hope you're well.
I hope your life gives you
Wonderful stories to tell.
I hope you have peace
At the end of the day,
And most of all,
I hope you hear me pray.

I hope you know that you are loved
In a way only a mother can,
And even though
You might not feel it,
I am always holding your hand.

I hope when you close
Your eyes at night,
Your mind is at rest.
I hope you have learned
To forgive others;
That's the only way
To truly gain rest.
But mostly, I hope
In your heart of hearts
That you know
You are only steps away
To opening the back door of your home
Where you once felt safe each day.

I hope you know that I love you
No matter the past and its woes,
For you will always be my only son—
That's how our story goes.

W I S H E S

I wish I could find my son somewhere
Hidden inside
The hard exterior of the man he is
Where a little boy used to reside.

I wish I could find
His bright brown eyes
And his big handsome smile.
I wish he could just sit and talk with me
If just for a little while.

I know he's in there somewhere,
The son I used to know—
The one who was my "tater tot"
Whom I always had in tow.

I wish my son could remember, like me,
The bond we used to share.
But for now, I just have memories
Of when he used to care.

TODAY'S THE DAY!

Today's the day I'm not going to cry.
Today's the day I'm not going to lie
To anyone
About how you don't even try
To be in my life.

Today's the day I'm not looking back.
Today's the day I'm losing track
Of the days, the months, and yes, the years
We lack!

Today's the day I'm taking flight
To enjoy life
Without you.

Today's the day I'm going to be there
For the people in my life who truly care.
For without them, whom could I share
My moments, my doubts, my goals, my fun?
You surely can't be the one.

Today's the day I'm not going to miss you.
There are still many things I want to do—
With or without you.
I'm not going to lie around and miss today
Just because you refuse to say
What I did that's not okay.

Today's the day I lose all thoughts of "why."
Today's the day I'm not going to cry.
I know this sounds so grown-up and strong,
But that's where you all are so very wrong.

THEN COMES
THE MORNING

And then came the morning;
It came without warning.
It slipped through the blinds
And the curtains of my mind.

At first, it was blinding,
This light that I sought.
It warmed my senses till no more I fought.
I climbed out of bed without hesitation.
I felt a new purpose,
A new determination.

Where have you been, my friend?
I've missed your strength
And the promise you hold
Of a new day
And a new story to behold.

I've been in the grip of the night and its darkness
For all too long.
The morning's light brings hope
Back to where it belongs.

WALKING ON EGGSHELLS

Walking on Eggshells is a skill
I've learned to achieve.
It's similar to *not* wearing
Your heart on your sleeve.

If you haven't figured
this out yet,
This is not meant to be.
Walking around on tippytoes
Trying not to concede
to what you really want to say
and to what you really mean.

It's not my way to be seen
And not heard.
But then why have I been invited?
To sit in the background
And not say a word?

Don't bother with your invites anymore,
If I'm just going to be ignored.
And feel as if
I'm being pushed out the back door.
No one puts Mama in the corner!
Wouldn't you agree?
I'd rather stay home alone than not be seen.

Start crushing those eggshells!
Quit looking over your shoulder.
You are worth so much more
Than a spot in the corner.

We deserve the best a child can give.
Not a life full of shame
For not knowing what we did.

PICTURES

I must have a hundred pictures
Of the son I used to know.
They cry from the walls and the hallway
And flow to the rooms down below.

From a tree, I see you swinging,
Your eyes so big and bright.
"Push me a little higher!" you yell
With all your strength and might.

Then I see a handsome young man
Wearing a cap and gown,
Family all around you,
Feeling mighty proud.

And there you are posing at the prom
Beside your best friend Dave.
He was the best at making us laugh.
Those are the times that I crave.
Oh, there you are at the door
Of your own first place.
You look so excited
As you anticipate
Starting college life with
Girls and beers and such.
We knew before you did,
You weren't going to study much!

Then there are the pictures of you
And your daughter,
The ones who speak to me like no other.
Where have you gone?
Where have you been?
It's been years now
Since you have asked me in.

Then there comes the question of
What I shall do.
Shall I take them all down
So I stop thinking of you?

But then, what am I saying
If you aren't there
On the mantle, on the dresser,
Or resting above my chair?
Does it mean I finally just don't care?

For those big brown eyes still follow me
From their places on the wall—
Eyes full of confidence,
Eyes full of joy,
Eyes telling me you were once
My little boy.

I guess I'm just not able
To believe you are really gone.
But I also realize after years of trying,
I have done nothing wrong.

The precious photos I see of you
Growing into a man
Have finally made me realize
We do the best we can!

GOODBYE TO PAIN

There's this thing called pain—
It starts in your brain.
It crawls down to your heart,
And there it remains.

Your heart becomes filled
With hurt and sadness
Until it seems it may burst
With the weight of its heaviness.

But then, there's a little beat of hope,
And you feel a release.
Your heart starts to open
To gather some peace.

The pain starts to lessen
As it flows through your limbs.
It's on its way out,
This hurt from within.

It radiates outward
Through your fingers and toes,
And soon, your heart beats quietly,
Letting you grow.

Don't give up, my friend.
Don't let this pain win.
It's starting its way out,
Limb by limb.

HEALING

I knew I was feeling better
When I started to sing.
It was like a baby bird
Teetering on its wing.

And then I started dancing
To songs that I love.
And I looked to the heavens
To thank God above.

I knew I was healing
One limb at a time.
My sorrow was drying out
One tear at a time.

I was shouting for joy.
I was shedding my skin.
I was becoming the person
I knew was within.

I stopped dwelling on the hurt
And the years I had lost,
Wondering what I did wrong
And the time it had cost.

I started to smile at the wonders
That abound
And stopped looking for you,
My child,
As I walked through our town.

I could feel my world open
To what I was missing.
My eyes started seeing;
My ears started listening.

And what I saw was a light
At the end of the road
Where people were laughing
At stories being told.

I saw the wonders of nature
As they are meant to be—
Rainbows and sunsets
And the almighty seas.

I heard myself laughing
With kids passing by
Where I used to turn away
Without a dry eye.

I know my soul is healing
From this grief I've embraced.
It came to me slowly;
At its own pace.

I wish this for you
As time goes on—
A revitalized life returned
Where once it was gone.

BABY STEPS

May your eyes be opened;
May your ears finally hear
The prayers I've said for you
Year after year.

May your arms be outstretched
To gather all my hugs.
May you remember someday soon
How much you are loved.

May your legs never grow weary
In this life that you tread.
May you always have a resting place
To lay your weary head.

May your thoughts of me be good ones.
May your footsteps show the way.
And may you find the courage
To open my door someday.

It would just take baby steps
To break through my pain,
To bring the joy back into my life
And start over again.

Can't we just take those baby steps?

THROUGH THE
KITCHEN WINDOW

Through the kitchen window,
I see memories passing by
Of a new baby's diapers
Hanging on the clothesline.

Of a little boy wobbling down
Our long sidewalk,
Trying not to sway,
Past the old swing set
Where once kids used to play.

Of a swing that hung on our huge maple tree
When all the world seemed so carefree.
I see boys playing basketball
Under that tree
And cars being washed
And tents being tossed.

I see my dad raking leaves
In our back lot
And jumping in each pile
Were my son and his dog.

I see balls of every kind
And a little wading pool,
And picnics replaced
Our long days in school.

I see boys playing whiffle ball
And catch
And neighbors who were
The very best.
I see Pappy's truck, Big Red,
And Easter egg hunts behind the shed.

I remember huge snow piles
Where kids have tumbled down
And bikes and scooters
Lying all around.

And grandchildren have visited
From close by and afar.
I cherish each one,
No matter where they are.

My view through the kitchen window
Has changed each year.
But the wonderful memories I have
Will always stay near.

YOU HAVE WON!

I awoke this morning with the sun
Shining through.
The birds are still singing;
The sky is still blue.
So what am I going to do?

Am I going to lie here
And feel sorry for myself?
The sun is saying,
"Wake up,
And start anew!"
Don't miss this gorgeous day
That's been waiting on you.

Don't miss out again on nature's display.
Forget your struggles, and enjoy the day.
The leaves are still changing,
As they always do.
Nature is not going to wait on you.

Call your best friend;
Take a drive.
Breathe in God's earthly scents,
And come alive!

When you feel the sadness
Starting to grow,
Pinch yourself,
And let your senses flow.

I know what you're thinking:
Easier said than done.
But you are a winner,
A survivor—
You have won!

HOLIDAYS

Why do I feel so empty
When the holidays are near?
I want to feel like the rest of the world
And be filled with the joy
Of the new year.

I want to open my eyes
And be excited
On that blessed Christmas morn,
Jump out of bed with delight,
And behold the day He was born.

I want to rejoice in family
And greet them with love and cheer.
But I know some will be absent,
And it will be hard to hold back my tears.

But this holiday will be different.
I'm going to embrace
Those whom I love
And remember those who have passed
And are looking down from above.
There are those who have no one
At this jolliest time of year.
I feel very blessed to be among
The ones whom I hold dear.

Sing with the holiday music
You've come to know and love.
Dance as you decorate your home
The way you've always done.

Make a bunch of cookies
Just to smell that smell.
Before you know it,
Your heart will begin to swell.

And maybe, just maybe,
You'll forget to be sad.
Enjoy the busyness of the holidays,
And forget why you were mad.

Traditions will always be there to comfort you
When your busy day is through.
Strive to reinvent them,
Or start something new.
My hope for you is peace
As you struggle to enjoy these days.
Treasure those who love you,
And dance those blues away.

ABOUT THE AUTHOR

IClaire is a retired elementary school teacher with 36 years of experience. She ended her career with a Masters degree in Elementary Education and graduated with a minor in English. During her teaching career she wrote for a teacher's publication in which teachers found both humor and pertinent information in those times about education. While teaching, she especially enjoyed working with the students on writing and publishing their own books. The author also enjoyed writing raps, songs, and poetry that the students would perform during assemblies or talent shows. More recently Claire has become interested in the complexity of estrangement and how it effects the core of a family. She began writing poetry to ease her own personal grief and has decided to share her poetry with others. She has one son, three stepdaughters, and five grandchildren. She lives with her husband in a small village in Pennsylvania. They enjoy the beach, traveling, and antiquing together.

CPSIA information can be obtained
at www.ICGtesting.com
Printed in the USA
LVHW030935010221
677996LV00021B/708